TREASURE FROM
THE EDGE OF ETERNITY

TREASURE
FROM THE
EDGE OF
ETERNITY

*Stories from Those Who've Sailed
Over the Horizon*

T. DURANT FLEMING

Hardy, Arkansas
Summer 2022

Charleston, SC
www.PalmettoPublishing.com

Paperback ISBN: 979-8-88590-661-6
eBook ISBN: 979-8-88590-662-3

I remember asking my father, who was gravely ill, knowing he would never leave the hospital, "Dad, how are we today?" Without opening his eyes, he quipped, "I'd rather be sailing."

Contents

"Teach us to number our days carefully so that we may develop wisdom in our hearts."
—Psalm 90:12

Nobody Gets off This Planet Alive—The Time to Live Is Now

This book should have been written twenty years ago, but the timing just wasn't right. Some things are just that way. The reality is that I did not write this book; scores of others wrote it for me. They gave it to me, and I considered their gift to be among the most precious things that I could ever receive. For some of them, the words and the wisdom they passed on to me would be one of the last acts that they would perform in this life. What does one do when given such a gift? It must be shared.

As an ordained minister of twenty-five years before I became a full-time educator, I found myself in all kinds of unique circumstances—performing happy weddings, visiting hopeless prisoners, laboring on politically dicey mission fields, celebrating births at hospitals, being present with families when loved ones where pronounced dead, enjoying sunny church picnics, helping others during the storm of horrendous divorces, and toasting the shared joys of good folks living in community. Yes, the ministry places you in some pretty rich and often challenging situations. It is as if you have a unique ringside seat at the Passing Parade of Life. It's like you have special access, a curious passport of sorts, into some of the more intimate, meaningful, and complex situations that the human condition has to offer.

As was mentioned earlier, this book was given to me, gifted to me by people who are now gone. They may have died, but from the perspective of faith, they are not actually gone, they have just sailed over the horizon. My occupation placed me in the most intimate proximity with those who were dying. At first, to be very honest, it was part of the job I detested. Talking to the dying, sitting next to them as their lives slipped away, the tearful families—it was just too taxing, too intimate, too painful. (If you think that ministers don't live in the real world and are shielded from the realities of life behind their clerical vestments, let me challenge you to do what they do for about six months. Chances are you'll gladly hand that job right back to them after experiencing some of the suffering and complex human situations that ministers encounter regularly.) As an unseasoned young minister, I found spending time with the dying almost overwhelming, but as the years slipped by, it became part of the normal process of life: we are born, we age, and eventually we die—spring, summer, fall, winter. Over the years, something changed in me, and I began to listen, sincerely listen, to what those whose lives were done were telling me. Their lessons were like gold that had been refined by a lifetime of thought, learning, struggle, hope, experience, family, failure, suffering, and joy. I began to tuck their words, these life-polished gems, away in my mind, understanding that these were precious artifacts for the living, treasure from the edge of eternity. Yes, I owe this book to dozens of great folks, good-hearted people who over the years honestly shared their lives with me in their final days, hours, and even minutes.

The longer I listened to the wisdom of the dying, the more I saw patterns emerge. Over time, I heard the same themes again and again. These were folks from all walks of life, yet there were common threads, like similar melodies, that were communicated. I began taking note of them, and as more years passed, they continued to be confirmed as these same topics continued to surface. There were several themes that repeated themselves; they overlapped with one another a bit, and like life, they often didn't fit in neat, tidy boxes. I began not only to ponder these themes, but I took them to heart and began to act upon them. To encounter the dying is to be challenged in some fundamental way. I found their counsel to be of such benefit that it led me to produce this project in order to share their words with others.

Finally, a few important thoughts before we move on to the next chapter. The principles presented within this book are ideals, universal truths, axioms for life. The last thing this author wants to project is that he has somehow mastered or perfectly acquired these lessons. Absolutely not. These lessons from the dying have been helpful and inspiring, but I have a long, long way to go before I can claim any command of these ideals (my wife of almost forty years can confirm this!). Life is a journey, and we travel this journey one step at a time.

Also, I hope you do not find this work overly grim due to its source, those who are dying. Modernity has significantly insulated us from death and dying, and it's to our loss. Years ago, a friend in the funeral home business told me about a son who called the funeral home and wanted his deceased mother cremated and then FedExed to him across the country. I'm guessing that he couldn't find the time in his schedule to personally oversee these final responsibilities, so the funeral home cremated the parent, packaged her up in a cardboard box, and shipped her out West to be placed on the porch of her very busy son. Yes, times have changed.

Today, death is almost viewed as something unnatural, obscene, something to be avoided. In the scope of human history, this is a relatively new phenomenon. Just two or three hundred years ago, whether the death was due to accident, disease, or age, friends and family gathered for the rich opportunity to say their farewells or to make amends if necessary. The dying had an opportunity to do the same, to say goodbye, patch up old wounds, and share what they believed to be important to the living. This often took place in the family home. Not so today. Hospitals with their many doors often have layers of security one must navigate in order to visit the dying. As a minister, I was able to gain access to patients others could not visit. And even then, in people's final moments, they might find themselves in a strange, sterile environment surrounded by clicking machines, fluorescent lights, and health-care workers who are complete strangers, rather than in the comfort of a warm home surrounded by relatives and loved ones. Thankfully, hospice is changing this scenario, helping families reconnect and become involved in the human process of dying. They are superheroes. Whenever you see a hospice worker, give them a genuine hug. It's not weird, they will understand.

I have heard it said that when a person dies, a library is lost forever. Being surrounded by loved ones gives the dying a chance to tell their stories, to pass on a small piece of their personal library so it won't be lost forever. Thankfully, many of the people with whom I had conversations did not die in isolation but surrounded by family and exceptional people who deeply understood the art of dying. As a result of this kind of support, I am passing on to you some of the timeless gems from their personal libraries—words that were not lost.

If you have ever been there, you know the last days or moments of a person's life are sacred. These moments are to be respected, even revered, set apart. As a minister, I learned that one must handle sacred things very carefully. Many of the things spoken to me by the dying were in private and in the context of trust. It is my chief goal of this short book to respect this. There are many things from those sacred moments that I will not be able to share, but I will attempt to communicate as best I can those things that I truly believe that those on their deathbeds would want you to know. Again, I want to preserve the spirit of the hallowed trust with which this information was given. The weight of doing this properly is what has made me balk at attempting to produce this book. However, I could not let these lessons slip into obscurity, so after many years of reflection, I picked up the pen. What I learned from the dying was just too practical, too helpful, and too inspiring not to pass along to others. To keep these things to myself would have been selfish, and for these stories to die with me would be a serious waste.

You will find that the lessons gleaned from my conversations with the dying are not sad or gloomy but actually affirming and genuinely helpful. As a matter of fact, as you will see within these pages, there was a lot of laughter and rare wit present in these final conversations. No, this is not a book about death; it is a book about life and how we might better live our lives while we still have time. Years ago, the presiding minister reminded the congregation at my father's funeral, "Nobody gets off of this planet alive." From time to time, we must be reminded of this, reminded to live now, to choose to live today. That is what this little book is about; it's about listening to the sagacious voices of those who have gone ahead of us. Their words will help us live, because the time to live is now.

The Voices behind This Book—
A Gift to the Living

Before we proceed, a bit more background might be helpful. As I have mentioned, I did not produce this book; it was actually a gift given to me by dozens of people over a span of many years. Yes, I sat down and put a pen to paper, but the critical thoughts within this book are not my own. I am merely a messenger, someone simply conveying the thoughts of others.

Who are these people, and why are their words so significant? All of the voices you will hear in regard to this project have passed on; they are all dead. Of course, I have shielded and altered their identities, but these were ordinary people, men and women just like yourself. They had jobs, families, and struggles and grappled with the same pressures of life with which we are all acquainted, yet it was the circumstances in which they found themselves that gave their words a particular potency, a certain gravity. They all knew they were dying, and for some, death was imminent.

The words of the dying have been given particular attention across the centuries. Many books have been compiled of the last recorded words of individuals as if these words were or are particularly helpful or poignant or special in some way. What is it about a person's last words? What is so unique about them? Why across the centuries have they been written down and passed along for generations as if they were holy writ or contain a special kind of wisdom? Are these final utterances somehow superior, or do they contain more significance than our daily conversations?

Having personally sat next to more than a few deathbeds, I would agree there is something special, very special, about what one says in one's last days and hours. This is difficult to articulate, but we know it's true. It is as if death is a great purifying crucible that somehow refines or distills one's thoughts. On one's deathbed, there is no more time for posturing or vagueness or pettiness or trivialities. Things are heavier, thicker, much more focused. It is as if death puts ego in its proper place and liberates one, even invites one, into a more honest or earnest state.

Strangely, during these moving conversations with the dying, I would often forget about time. The clock did not seem to matter. Time became very abstract. I'd leave the hospital and look at my watch and could not believe that hours had passed. Encountering death seemed to recalibrate things, resize things, and with an unspoken sense of urgent authority, it somehow put things in their right place. I would usually leave these meetings with death striving to be a better person. These stories still have that same effect on me.

While reading these stories, you may think at times, "That was not what I thought should happen" or "I am sure what I would do in that situation" or "I really hope something like that never happens to me." Good, that's the way death is; it is completely unconcerned about your sensibilities. Death never asks for permission. There is no negotiating. It is the great intruder. It has no regard for your daily routine, your future ambitions, your cherished relationships, your financial concerns, or your complicated situations in life. When death draws near, everything gives way. Everything.

Even though dying moments are weighted with pathos, thick with emotion, there is plenty of room for humor. I have laughed with families until the tears rolled as we stood around the bed of someone whose funeral was only a few days distant. I remember asking my father, who was gravely ill, knowing he would never leave the hospital, "Dad, how are we today?"

Without opening his eyes, he quipped, "I'd rather be sailing."

Like the Spartans who calmly combed their hair before battle in the presence of their enemies, humor in the face of death can be powerful and a profound form of expression.

Again, who were these folks whose voices and wisdom we will explore? Regular people in extraordinary situations, facing the conclusion of their lives. They were housewives, salesmen, military veterans, cancer patients,

the wealthy, and the not so wealthy. They were churchgo-
ers, nonchurchgoers, presidents of companies, and some
who had lost fortunes. Most were over fifty but not all. A
minister who has been with it for a while has buried cas-
kets of all sizes. Suffering never discriminates. They were
people who had great joys in this life and equally great
regrets. Some were surrounded by large, caring families
as they died; others were practically alone. Some had
lived a life of virtue and selfless service to others, while
others had painful and selfish dark pasts. Their hidden
secrets were betrayed by the deep lines on their faces.
Their eyes did not smile when their mouths did. Some of
the folks I met at the end of their time on earth went to
Ivy League schools; others did not make it through the
eighth grade. Some were diagnosed months in advance
of their funerals with a terminal condition, and we visited many times; others I met only once, and that was
in their final moments. In ministry, you do not have the
liberty to choose your clients. It is generally suffering,
that great equalizer, that establishes the relationship,
and suffering knows no strangers. In these pages, you
will meet all kinds of people, and you will hear their
insights as they face the inevitable.

I call the words that were spoken to me by these good
people a gift because that is exactly what they are. Some
of them I knew very well; in some cases, they were strangers until our lives crossed, and it was death that brought
us together. At times, I felt like I was an intruder, barging
into the most emotionally charged and personal episode
of their life on earth. I often felt unworthy to be present,

as if I had not earned the right to be there sharing these sacred moments with their family, but time and time again, I was graciously included. My life will never be the same. When I was a young seminarian, I thought that we the living are the ones who minister to the dying, and that is somewhat true, but across the decades, I have learned that the dying are the ones who often minister to us. If we listen to them, their life-forged wisdom will help us on this journey. But we must listen.

CHAPTER 1

Give Them Their Flowers before the Funeral—Loving Others Today

It had been about a week since I'd been to the hospital to visit Martha. During my fist visit, she was so tired that I spent most of the time speaking with her sister. Martha was a gracious elderly lady who lived just outside of Bolivar, Tennessee, and every time I saw her, she was doing two things, smiling and apologizing for the condition of her hair. Once while visiting Martha, I had this conscious thought, "Here is this lady who has only been given only a few weeks to live, and she is apologizing to me regarding the state of her hair!" On this particular day, she let me know that her hairdresser friend Bennie was coming that afternoon to spruce her up.

I had been to Martha's hospital room about three times by then, but this time, something was different, very different. As I entered the room, I saw it was completely filled with flowers and flower arrangements of all sorts. There were flowers on shelves, flowers on the bedside tables, flowers in the bathroom, and flowers covering much of the floor except for a path to her bedside and a path to the bathroom. I had never seen so many beautiful flowers of all colors and varieties in one room—forget a hospital room, in any room! It reminded me of those tiny, cramped flower shops in Manhattan, and on this visit, I remember the wonderful scent of gardenias. Upon entering Martha's floral-filled room, I looked around to take it all in; then I looked at Martha, who was wearing a wide, glowing grin. She had lost significant weight since our last visit.

"Look, Durant! They gave me my flowers before the funeral!"

Initially, I was flabbergasted. I was not sure how to respond to Martha's courageous declaration. In my seminary training, I had learned that in serious hospital and funeral home situations, if you are not sure what to say, don't say anything; just be there. Those situations are the very last places where you want to be planting your foot squarely into your mouth, so I just stood there smiling with my mouth open in admiration of both this hospital room stuffed with flowers and what she had just exclaimed: "They gave me my flowers before the funeral!"

What I did not know was that Martha was a life-long member of a small church where she had served in almost every capacity and was genuinely adored. That little church had seen many a pastor come and go, and it was Martha who was the devoted glue that held that community together. Knowing that she only had days to live, that church had lovingly ambushed her. They had organized and schemed to bring joy into her life by bringing her more flowers than would possibly fit into her hospital room. Leaving her room that day, I noticed the overflow, the full extent of that church's expression of love for Martha. The flowers poured out onto the floor of the hallway. There were flowers all around the nursing stations, flowers in the waiting room, and even flowers in the rooms of other surprised patients. I was not Martha's pastor, nor did I perform her funeral the following month. I was just a friend of an extended family member who sometimes went to the church where I was on staff, but that outpouring of affection and Martha's response has never left me. Encountering the dying is like a sacrament; it coaxes you toward change.

"They gave me my flowers before the funeral!" What a wonderful thought. What a lesson for us all. On one hand, it is a very simple, fiercely honest, unvarnished statement; on the other hand, it offers us a universal axiom, a helpful principle for us all. It encourages us not only to love one another but to be certain to express this love while we are still able, while there is still time. We ought not wait until tomorrow. Talk to any minister, and I can almost guarantee you that they will tell you that more than a few times, they have supported someone, often in tears, who was shouldering a heavy burden of regret. It is the regret of not taking the time or taking the risk to truly express their affection for a loved one who is now dead. This grief is often exceptionally deep because there is no going back, there is no turning back the clock, and there is no way to repair the issue. As frayed as a relationship may be, we the living still have the opportunity to reach out, to express ourselves, to sort it out. Death closes that door forever.

So, what do we do? Anything is better than nothing. Maybe it's time for us to write that letter that we keep putting off or make that phone call to let our father know that we truly appreciate and love him or schedule that lunch with a child just to tell them how awesome they are or purchase that special gift for a friend to say, "You need to know how special you are to me." I remember when I was about sixteen, watching a good friend of my father after dinner and cordials give my father a very fine Belgian-made shotgun. It was a concrete expression of a lifelong friendship. Intentions are wonderful, but action is what really matters. The time to give others their flowers before the funeral is today, before death without warning forever slams that door shut.

And just for the record, the last time I saw Martha, her hair looked fabulous.

CHAPTER 2

Live Now—Time Is Not
on Our Side

The door opened before I even had a chance to ring the doorbell. This well-groomed, king-sized home in East Memphis was the kind of house you'd see in a slick magazine. I was greeted by a classically attractive, well-garbed woman who appeared to be in her mid-seventies. Introducing herself in that delightful Southern way, she motioned for me to enter her magazine-worthy home. As we stepped down from the dark, slate-decked entrance hall, we entered into a spacious sunken den. I then quickly noticed that the room had been reconfigured, transformed in order to meet the needs of the man I had come to see. That spacious den was now this man's tidy bedroom with everything that a person dying of cancer may need. I had never met these kind folks before, but I was scheduled to preside over this gentleman's funeral; we just didn't know when.

"Take a seat here. Can I get you some coffee or a glass of water?"

"No thank you, but thank you."

"Let me get out of y'all's way," said the wife, who could have been a movie star back in the sixties, "so y'all can get to know each other." She then deftly disappeared down a hallway filled with a lifetime of photographs. This was a unique situation and potentially a very awkward one to be sure. The gentleman reclined in what appeared to be a hospital-type bed, and like his wife, he was very well dressed. As he rested atop the bed's covers, I noticed his finely-stitched leather house shoes, his well-fitted pajamas, and his handsome robe that looked more like a smoking jacket. He was clean-shaven with his hair carefully combed. He too looked like a movie star; all he needed was a long cigarette holder. He was square-jawed and possessed a military bearing. When he spoke, he peered straight into my eyes. It was nearly uncomfortable, but this feeling was overcome by his infectious smile. I could tell instantly that this man was a natural leader, a straight-talker, a no-nonsense kind of guy, and in the next few moments, I discovered that I could not have been more accurate in my assessment.

His first words were "So you're the guy who's going to bury Bull Thompson! Word has it that the senior pastor at the church, the Big Cheese, will likely be out of pocket for the funeral, so I drew you, the 'B team' minister."

As I scrambled for words, he quickly broke the growing tension with a toothy grin and a candid laugh. "I'm just pulling your leg. Relax. I'm the one dying here!" This guy was something else.

This is a good time for a brief, literary side road. During pastoral training in seminary, one learns to develop a fundamental skill when making visitations. You always attempt to match the tonality of the circumstances in which you find yourself—you don't laugh when people are crying, you avoid being somber at joyous occasions, and you're not glib during solemn moments. It's not rocket science, but it does require some circumspection. A seasoned pastor understands how subtle and complex some situations can be. Once at a social event, I jingled the ice in my glass as I spoke with a young woman. In an instant, she grew gravely serious. "Will you please stop doing that?" That was all I needed to know to understand that she had probably suffered at some point in her life as a result of alcohol abuse. We humans are complicated.

When I entered the Thompson home that fall day, I knew that Bull Thompson was dying, that I was designated to perform his funeral, and that he only had a few weeks to live according to his doctors. I entered that space mentally prepared to manage a pretty heavy situation, but this was not at all what I experienced upon my arrival. He seemed to be happy, full of energy, and incredibly frank. He had the knack of using sternness as a setup for humor the way a skilled golfer sets up the golf ball on the tee. He was actually playing off the fact that he was dying to toy with me a bit. I was completely impressed with his absolute candor and his audacious sense of humor. So, I shifted gears, relaxed, and began to laugh. We had a memorable afternoon. I had never seen anyone approach death with so much life.

Bull expressed no interest in planning his funeral. Pointing at me with his index finger, "Y'all are clergy. It's what y'all do. You are a professional, and I'm sure it will be just fine."

The only thing he requested was a brief graveside service. Nothing fancy, nothing sad, nothing drawn out, and definitely nothing mushy. Amused, I assured him that as a former Anglican, I could certainly perform a liturgically based, short, semidry, non-mushy service. He got a kick out of that. I then asked him if it was OK to speak to his wife about her thoughts on the funeral at another time, knowing she probably had her own ideas about the service, and if my read on this couple was accurate, Caroline usually got what she wanted. Again, I could not believe how energetic he was and how much clarity he possessed. As far as the oncologists were concerned, he was about to cross the River Styx, and yet he appeared to be challengingly jovial and quite animated.

Bull went on to share why he called me to come to his home. Understandably, he just wanted to get to know me because I was going to be the one who would be there with his family, as we "lowered him into the ground." So, we visited for nearly three hours, talking about family, faith, and fly-fishing, among other things. Finally, and I had anticipated this, Caroline graciously reentered the room and with a smile kindly told Bull that it was time for his afternoon rest. Before I could stand to begin the exiting process, (in the South, you don't just leave someone's home; you continue to visit toward the door, and once outside, you continue to visit on the porch and then toward your car. Plans are being made to visit again for dinner in the near future. It's a wonderfully complex Southern ritual, a form of social dance). Bull leaned over, took me firmly by the arm, and in a solemn tone that I had not met that day, asked me squarely, "Where did the time go? I was just fifteen the other day. I was in college moments ago. Our wedding was just the other day. Durant, where did it go? Where did my life go? It all happened so quickly. So fast! So damn fast! I cannot believe my life is over." He continued, "I can handle the fact that we are all born, we grow old, and we die...no problem there...That's what we signed up for...I was just not prepared for how fast it would happen."

Without breaking eye contact with this strong-willed gentleman, I nodded slowly, not to indicate that I fully understood, but to acknowledge that I had clearly heard what he was saying and that his words would not be forgotten. I have not forgotten; his words have not been lost. They are now yours.

I worked very hard to make sure that Bull's funeral was just the way he would have liked it—brief, well-organized, a tad parched, uncomfortably frank, nothing maudlin, and of course sprinkled with some surprisingly direct humor. If Bull could have attended his own funeral, I think he would have said something like, "What are these people doing here standing around in the middle of the day? Don't they have something to do, somewhere to go? Y'all all need to get back to work! Go! Go back to work!" If my memory is correct, and I think it is, I believe

I even shared this at the funeral. He was one of a kind. What a character.

In 1963, the famous hit producer and American song-writer Jerry Ragovoy wrote the famous, soulful song, "Time Is on My Side." The song was first picked up by jazz trombonists, Kia Winding, then recorded again by soul artist, Irma Thomas (and of course later made famous by the Rolling Stones). The obvious irony surrounding this song is that everyone involved with the initial production and launch of this legendary tune is gone. They are all dead. How time marches on. If history has taught us anything about being human, it is that time is definitely *not* on our side. In broad historical terms, our lives occupy but a few minutes on humanity's expansive time line; in geological terms, we walk this earth for just a handful of seconds; and in light of the cosmos, we barely ever existed. As St. James wisely teaches us in his epistle, "Our lives are but a vapor."

What are we to do with this lesson, that time is precious, a limited commodity that cannot be halted or retrieved, and it is hurdling by at the speed of life? How are we to rightly respond to the earnest words of Bull, "Where did my life go? I was just fifteen years old the other day. It has all gone by so fast! So damn fast!" What do you think? What is your response? Will this goad us into thinking or acting any differently? Personally, I think our best response would be to strive to be consciously present wherever we may be, to live "in the now," to live intentionally now, right now. This seems to be more of an attitude, more of a state of mind, than an activity. It appears that the art of living now is more about quality than quantity, more about depth than length of life.

This is much more than producing an ambitious bucket list, which can actually woo us into longing for those future activities rather than focusing on the now. We can easily fall into the trap of always planning or living in the future in such a way that we do not fully savor or celebrate the present. Future considerations may well diminish the beauty and deliciousness of right now. If we take living in the now to heart, it may actually change us. We might just be more observant, more patient. We might just be more thoughtful, we might truly listen to others, we might just slow down to enjoy the simplest of things, and we might even begin to smile at some of the stuff that really used to annoy us. As we go about today, whatever that means, let's attempt to live right here, right now. We are wise to remember Bull's words, that one day for certain, we will run out of time.

Time is not on our side.

CHAPTER 3

Drink More Champagne—
Celebration as a Virtue

ntering his room, I noticed that Harold didn't even attempt to smile. He was tired and back in the hospital for more tests. He had considered telling his three adult daughters that there were going to be no more tests. He was going to let them know with finality that he was done with them, but the gray, aging, gaunt man didn't have the energy to wage that battle. He knew he was outnumbered anyway.

"Harold, it's good to see you again. Back in for more tests?"

Harold used the bed's remote control to sit up a bit. "Yep, more tests. Always, more tests." I had spent some time with this well-known businessman about a month earlier, in the same hospital room. He was in for a battery of medical tests. Harold, a well-liked, multigenerational Memphian, had spent his entire life in the cotton business. Because of our age difference, I did not know Harold directly, but this was one of those Southern "my people knew your people" situations, so by association, there was a certain comfort level we enjoyed. He had worked for his family's business during the summers while in high school, and he just never stopped. He was such a benefit at the shop that he just stopped going to high school one day, and no one really said anything about it. It seemed like the reasonable thing to do. Over time, he had held virtually every position at the firm and knew every jot and tiddle about the industry. Harold's vast knowledge of the business was only surpassed by his indomitable work ethic. He was raised by Depression-era survivors. During that time, his struggling family had held on tightly to one another, and by force of will as well as some really good luck, they survived that economic hurricane. For better or for worse, that event made a permanent impression on a young man who would work tirelessly for the rest of his life to ensure that he and his family would never have to go without ever again. He worked with something akin to a holy anger.

Although Harold was kind and soft-spoken, do not let that fool you; the man was made out of titanium. The Depression had forged him into a machine. He was always the first to work and the last to leave, and there was nothing at the shop that he would not do. This elderly business owner would often be seen after hours taking out trash, sweeping the floors, or double-checking invoices. He personally signed and gave birthday cards for every employee with a few twenties enclosed. He was an inspiration to everyone who worked with him, not because of what he said, but because of what he did.

He was definitely an "actions speak louder than words" kind of guy.

Even in his early eighties, he could quietly outwork anyone in the building. Although he exuded the relaxed nature of a Southern gentleman, never wearing a tie, walking with a long gait, smiling in a way that set folks at ease, if you worked for Harold, you had better bring your best efforts every single day. He viewed slacking off, blame-shifting to reduce one's responsibilities, or putting off today's work until tomorrow as grave moral wrongdoings. If you worked for Harold, you never said, "That's not my job." He believed that every task in the building was everyone's collective responsibility. Quality was to be owned by everyone. Many a cocky college intern lasted only about a fortnight at the firm because it usually took them about that long to figure out what they had actually gotten themselves into—very hard, challenging work. Back in the sixties, Harold hung a large, red-and-white hand-painted sign in a common area that could be seen by every employee every day. It was that famous quote by Thomas Edison, a personal hero of Harold's: "Opportunity is missed by most people because it is dressed in overalls and looks like work." That was Harold's credo; that was who he was.

In his prime, Harold was like an unstoppable force of nature, but time does what time does, and now his eyes were dim, his body was frail, and others were running the business. He often wondered but never asked if his old sign was still keeping watch over the workers in the common area.

"Harold, I just thought I'd check in, to see how you are doing and to see if you need anything."

He instantly retorted with a wry smile, "Yes, I do need something. You can get me the hell out of here!"

I told him that I was no match for his three red-haired daughters, who were standing guard, and if you know anything about strong Southern ladies, you know what I am talking about. There was absolutely no chance of liberating Harold from the gauntlet of medical tests he now faced, so that day, we spent the afternoon visiting, just talking about this and that.

That day, I had sneaked him some black licorice, the real old-school stuff, the kind he really liked. I discreetly slipped him the small white paper bag that I had picked up at the Roasted Peanut Shop on Summer Avenue. Taking the bag, he craned his head around toward the door to see if his daughters were watching; then he quickly dug into the bag and began chewing on a piece of the black candy. We had to be careful. One of his protective daughters had thoroughly chastised both of us during Harold's last hospital visit, claiming that my gift of Harold's favorite candy had screwed up his potassium levels. We pleaded innocent. Now, to Harold's delight, I had to smuggle in his licorice.

"Blood tests be damned," he mused, closing his eyes as he savored another piece of the black contraband. We sat in silence as he happily chewed away.

"I didn't drink enough champagne."

I had no idea what Harold was talking about; this statement came completely out of the blue. He stared blankly at the wall as he spoke; it was as if he was re-membering something.

"Yes...I didn't drink enough champagne." The chewing continued.

"I'm not sure I understand, Harold." My immediate thought was that he wanted me to run the blockade of his daughters again and smuggle up a bottle of champagne. "I worked too hard. I missed too much. I regret more than a few of the choices I made because of work."

I just listened.

"We had nice things, a nice home. No one ever went without, but the cost was great, maybe too great."

Now I understood where he was going.

"We rarely went on vacations. I missed plays, dance recitals, anniversary dinners, parties, and birthdays. Looking back, I was doing it *for* the family, but I was also doing it *to* the family."

Now he was talking with his hands as he spoke to the wall.

"There was a genuine cost, and I can't go back." Still staring at the wall, he said, "I should have relaxed more, spent more, listened more, traveled more, and enjoyed more. Now that I think about it—and this is awful to admit—I cannot remember dancing with my wife...I know I did...but I can't remember." Turning from the wall to me, he said, "I had a lot of success, but we did not celebrate it. I was always thinking of work, of the business, all of the time. I was late to Jill's wedding rehearsal. I was taking care of an important loose end at the shop. That night, everyone acted like it was not a big deal. It was a big deal...a real big deal." Wiping his eyes with the back of his hands, Harold confessed, "The truth is that I had forgotten about it. On that day, work was more important."

As a minister, now is when you just get out of the way and let a person talk, and Harold did.

After that visit, I never saw Harold again, but I will always remember his confession: "I didn't drink enough champagne." One of the hardest-working people I've ever met, he had it all but regretted that he did not slow down enough to enjoy his family and his only life, which was now at its conclusion. He had not celebrated life's goodness. That day, he confessed that he had not savored life's simple and special moments the way he savored that black licorice on his deathbed. Harold teaches us that now is the time to laugh. Now is the time to taste. Now is the time to dance. Now is the time to celebrate. Celebrate life now.

CHAPTER 4

Don't Sweat the Small Stuff— Keeping It in Perspective

I found myself grasping the wheel much tighter than usual. The two-lane highway was now covered in snow mixed with sleet. I would rather not be making this trip into the hill country of Northern Mississippi. It was a few days before Christmas, and I would have preferred to be at home, next to my warm fireplace, admiring our Christmas tree, sipping an old-fashioned, and watching SEC football. Then as I considered my destination as well as my duties for the day, all selfish thoughts washed away. I knew this young couple well, but I had never seen where "their people are from" as we say down South. That was why I was driving at dawn on this small, slick highway, heading to this out-of-the-way town where their people were from. Where was this tiny town? About eighty years south of Memphis.

As my tires crunched onto the gravel parking lot, I noticed that I was only the second car at the church. The first car was that of a deacon who came to turn on the heat and the lights. He met me on the front steps of the tiny church, and after we quickly exchanged pleasantries, the cold drove us inside.

"I better get some salt on these steps."

We both held fast onto the metal railing as we carefully negotiated the icy steps and then moved into the already warmed vestibule. As the deacon went for the rock salt, I sat in complete solitude, wedged into a creaky wooden chair just outside of the oddly shaped sanctuary. I worked to collect my thoughts. This was not going to be easy. After a quick prayer for strength, I just stared at the foot-worn maroon carpet of the vestibule. I did not want to be here—actually no one wanted to be here.

Soon people began to arrive. Another deacon, a large woman carrying a red choir robe, and relatives of all sorts entered the small church communicating in low tones. I heard the crunching of the gravel again and again as more cars arrived in the bad weather. There is no script in these situations; you just pray and wade right into them. By then, I was standing, holding open the church's door, greeting complete strangers in a completely strange place while all along watching for Bill and Katherine Marshall, the couple I had come to support. As they, with arms around one another, came in out of the sleet, we hugged, and I immediately ushered them to a small, quiet parlor that was off to the right side of the small sanctuary. They did not need to be swarmed by caring parishioners, former Sunday school teachers, and the large, well-meaning soloist. There would be plenty of time for that, just not right now. With tissues in hand, we spoke in that musty parlor with the lime-green carpet for what seemed like a half an hour. We prayed, and then I excused myself to make sure everything was prepared—the organist, the soloist, and the ushers.

Having done this before, I knew this required a deliberate mental and emotional shifting of gears, but it had to be done. I left the couple in the parlor with a few immediate family members, letting them know that I would be right back. I reviewed the order of service with the bearded organist, double-checked with the timing of the solos, and delivered to the pulpit a small stack of note cards containing my message for the service.

It was then that I came face to face with what had brought me to this remote country church. Positioned squarely in front of the well-worn pulpit was a casket, a small one, not even three feel long. I intentionally looked at the wooden casket to begin to acclimate myself to what was about to happen. Then, I just as intentionally looked away from it. I had much to do, and now was not the time to come unglued. A minister's duties are incredibly varied, more than most people know. There are unseen administrative duties, serious budget responsibilities, staffing pressures, wrangling with committees, endless sermon preparations, civic duties, attendance worries, choir mutinies for a new director, hospital visitations, threats of weird lawsuits, complicated weddings, and the never-ending avalanche of counseling. But talk to any pastor, and they will tell you burying a child, without question, is the most difficult pastoral service that can be performed. I hope I never see another tiny casket as long as I live.

The crowded service went well. It was short, heartfelt, and filled with both pathos and the immovable promises of God. Having small chdren myself at the time made this funeral particularly difficult, so much so that I had to emotionally disassociate myself at times. It is a form of mental dislocation. The deacons were very helpful, and the skilled organist did not miss a cue. Together, we all made it through that difficult morning, and as I drove back toward Memphis, I could not help but replay that mother's words over in my head. On that lonely drive back north, I counseled with myself that I would always remember what I had heard in the small parlor with that awful green carpet on that icy morning.

"I always wanted everything to be just right, to have a perfect family...Now I feel terrible, just terrible...I was too hard on Allie [sobbing]. I'd get frustrated when she'd lose a shoe, scold her when she spilled her juice [sobbing]...I spanked her just for playing with the channel changer... angry when she got too noisy...If I only had her back... if I only had her back, I'd do better, I know I'd do better...(Her words became screeches twisted by grief.) "She drew on the wall once..." She couldn't finish the sentence.

These things were hard to hear.

This story was so difficult for me to recall that I seriously considered omitting it from this book, but the lesson speaks loudly to us, the living. Katherine would have given anything to have her little girl back to lose a shoe, to play with the channel changer, and to draw on the wall. Perfection can be a cruel master, and if we are honest, we know in our hearts that much of life has ragged edges. There is a certain patina to life. It has built-in imperfections, scratches, and cracks that must be understood and accepted. Katherine's desire for perfection, to have everything "just right," had her striving against the grain of the way things are. To advance this thought a bit further, the imperfect patina of this life needs not only to be accepted but to be wisely embraced, for it is without a doubt woven inextricably into the rest of our journey on earth. If we do not grasp this, we will continue to sweat the small stuff, which generally leads to frustration and diminished joy.

The Navajo understood this. They would purposely weave imperfections into their rugs. It is called "Ch'ihónít'I," meaning "spirit path." It was a bold way of saying that only God is perfect, and we must embrace the reality that we are not. What a concept! Go ahead and accept your limitations and understand that life is not without imperfections. Generally, the older we get, the more we are forced by circumstances to acknowledge the imperfections of life, but we also know that there is no switch we can flip or pill we can take that completely delivers us from sweating the small stuff. It is something we can work on though. It is something we can practice, and over time, we might experience that frustrating dent in our car, the exasperating forgetfulness of our children, or the annoying idiosyncrasies of our spouse in a very different way. The Navajo would teach us to be thankful that we even have a car to be dented, to be grateful that we have wonderful children who are forgetful just like we are, and to smile that you have a fascinatingly unique spouse who is your partner in this life. Yes, embracing imperfections is something we must practice, and with practice, maybe, just maybe, we will find more joy.

CHAPTER 5

A Brief Reflection: The Cost of This Little Book—Lest We Forget

The ministry will teach you many things. As I mentioned earlier, it gives one a front-row seat to this thing called life. It can be so rich, so full of pathos, so unfiltered that one needs to take a break. Often when a minister goes on a sabbatical, it's not a nicety; it is a necessity if they are going to stay mentally, spiritually, and physically healthy. During World War I, before the advancements of modern psychology and our present-day understanding of PTSD, when a soldier emotionally just could not continue, it was labeled with the broad term *battle fatigue*. In ministry, the broad term is *burnout*. It is a reality that most people do not understand, and it needs to be clinically explored. A human being can only take so much, and most ministers will experience this state called burnout in varying degrees at some point in their careers. Many people believe that being a pastor is a cushy profession. I once heard a crotchety old church officer complain one morning as I arrived on a weekday to the church around midmorning, "Look whose dragging in late! Man, I wish I was a minister. You can show up late and only work one hour a week on Sundays." (Yes, a person actually said that.) I just waved, kept my mouth shut, and continued walking to my office. What that old geezer did not know was that I was up all night at the local hospital on a snowy evening with a young couple who had just lost their first child. That was only the second time that I had heard the animalistic wailing of a mother completely possessed by grief. I got home at dawn.

Why am I telling you this? Because this small book came at a cost, a terrific human cost. I was there. I experienced it. The helpful principles within these pages, these little diamonds, were formed under the extreme pressures of life. I am not drawing attention to this to make anyone feel guilty or to attempt to amplify their significance; it's just the truth. These pithy stories and the lessons they confer are pricy gifts from some really good people who have gone ahead of us. I can close my eyes and still see Martha's smile, hear Katherine's twisted voice, smile with Bull's toothy grin, and feel Harold's drive and passion. I can still hear them, and now you can hear them too. So, I believe the proper response should be gratitude and remembrance—gratitude for the diamonds they left behind, remembering that they were folks just like us on life's majestic journey.

CHAPTER 6

You Can't Take It with You— Avoiding Cumber

He was at the top of his game, in his mid-forties. Everything was clicking. All of his education and hard work were now bearing fruit. Stephen was one of those guys that you almost had to like, strikingly handsome, cleverly self-effacing, exceedingly sharp, physically fit, a Notre Dame graduate with a gorgeous family and a smile that made you smile. As an accomplished golfer, he had made more than a few holes in one. Things just went that way for him. Then he got sick, really sick.

When I entered Stephen's hyper sterile hospital room, his appearance had so changed that I had to make an effort to conceal my shock. He was now gaunt and moved about slowly, a shadow of his former athletic self. Due to his intensive treatment, he had lost all of his hair but not his smile. His smile still made me smile. "Hey, Durant, thanks for coming by." As he was fumbling around trying to open a small plastic container of orange juice, he said, "You know you guys, you ministers, make me nervous. When you guys start coming around a lot, I don't take that as a good sign." Not knowing what to say, I didn't say anything and just smiled. "Nah, I am just messing with you. I am glad you're here." Handing me the orange juice, he asked, "Can you open this. I can't get it open."

That day, we just visited, nothing important. I had just dropped by to say hello. Looking back, I realize I had no idea how sick Stephen really was. His smile, his unbridled optimism, his personable way, coupled with the hope that he might turn a corner, masked the reality that he would not be with us much longer. On that day, Stephen shared some of his trials along with some of the things that he was learning through his ordeal. "When I get out of here, I am going to do something differently."

"Like what?"

"I am smack in the middle of what some call 'the backbreaking years.' Those years in your thirties and forties when you are professionally crushing it. You are juggling eighty-hour workweeks, a family with small kids; you're doing whatever it takes to establish a nice home with nice things, and you are just hemorrhaging money in every direction. Also, for years, I've been in this 'acquisition phase' of life, and it's one heck of a treadmill." Now energized, he continued, "Go, go, go...earn more, buy more, earn more, buy more. When I get out of here, I swear I'm getting off of the treadmill. Who needs more of this stuff anyway? How many cars, how many houses, how many watches, how many Jet Skis, a gunite swimming pool, private schools, another set of golf clubs... Please don't get me wrong. I am blessed way more than I deserve, but I'm tired, tired of it all. Do we really need all of this stuff? I feel like I've just been chasing stuff for most of my life...Durant, am I making any sense?"

"Yes, yes, you are."

"Trust me, being in here gives you plenty of time to think. Paying for all of that stuff just keeps you on the treadmill, and I am tired. I am done with the treadmill. I'm done with it! Done with it!" In his enthusiasm, he made the same gesture that an umpire would make when someone is barely safe at home plate. Always measured and always even-tempered, Stephen checked himself, smiled, and reached for another small container of orange juice.

The Quakers have a name for it; they call it "cumber." Historically they worked hard to live simply, deliberately, purposefully so as not to take on too much cumber. The word means "burden" or "hindrance" or "obstruction." There is nothing wrong with having nice things until they become a burden or an obstruction to our joy or peace of mind. Stephen, whose mind was like a razor, shared with me that day about the obvious irony regarding the treadmill upon which he found himself. He was working so hard to provide for his family everything they needed, yet now they had everything they needed except for him. Illness often gives us a clarity that we did not ask for. It had revealed to Stephen that it was time for him to become unencumbered, unburdened by material pursuits and material things. It was time to focus upon his family and his quality of his life rather than a continued dedication to the acquisition of more.

If you want to do something to honor the memory of Stephen, that handsome young man with the contagious smile who loved the Fighting Irish, step off the treadmill. Do it. He was never able to follow through on his convictions—he ran out of time—but we can learn from him. We can live larger by buying less, enjoy the quality of things apart from the quantity of things, happily give some of our things away, and always put people first. Let's do it. Let's do it for Stephen. And one last thing, when you think of him, smile.

CHAPTER 7

Faith Matters—Death Be Not Proud

They called him Big Jake. In his mid-eighties, hunched over by age, he was now as bowlegged as a cow boss. Although he stood at only about five feet six inches tall, everything about Jake was big. He had big ideas, a big family, a big heart, and big faith. Despite his stature, he was an exceptionally large person, one of those rare personas that would naturally fill up whatever space they entered. Being around Jake was an experience. He was unusually perceptive. You had better not try to be someone you were not around him; he'd sniff that out and then address it quite frankly with a caring smile. Again, being around Big Jake was encouraging yet challengingly unorthodox. It was as if his deep faith and his eighty plus years of an exceptionally full life had distilled this man, forged this man, purified him in some way, into the wonderfully no-nonsense, gracious chainsaw that he was. I have never met anyone like him, and I have abandoned the thought that I ever will. As a barnstormer in his mid-twenties, he daringly flew his biplane under the Memphis-Arkansas Bridge at Memphis on the Mississippi River, and he never lost that pure gusto for life.

When he was way too old to be driving, he pulled into the parking lot of the church where I was on staff as the executive minister. In a previous conversation, Jake had said that he was going to visit me one day to tour the church, but I just thought it was a Southern nicety. I truly did not think he'd show up unannounced. He did. When I looked out of my office window and saw Big Jake, wearing an oversized polyester blazer and a really wide tie from the seventies, slowly extricating himself from his aging vehicle, I muttered to myself, "Oh my, here we go!" There were a lot of unknowns when you were around Jake. A lot of unscripted things could happen. He had a mind of his own, and you never knew where that might go. One night while at a restaurant with a group, I was tasked to find Jake, He had disappeared. I finally located him in the kitchen curiously talking with the dishwashing staff about how their newfangled washing machine functioned. When you were with Jake, you were not in control, and he would confess that he was not in control either. He called it Providence.

I hustled outside, took him by the arm, and escorted him into the church. As we moved past the secretarial staff, of course he let the ladies know how beautiful they all were. Hearing the happy commotion, our gracious senior pastor stepped out his office and joined us. "How are you? Jake, it's so good to have you visiting with us today!"

With no hesitation, Big Jake took a moment to size up the tall, well-dressed, well-spoken pastor. "Well, hello. Are you born again?"

"Yes. Yes, sir. Yes, sir, I am."

Jake nodded. "Good, good, too many pastors of these big churches are just businessmen running businesses. Good, that's good." He then turned to me. "Durant, show me around." Classic Big Jake.

Jake was as indomitable as he was loving. He had the closest personality type that I have met to that of the apostle Paul, tough but loving, weathered but energetic, gracious but fiercely honest. As a Gideon, Jake would go downtown to the Memphis prison to visit the inmates and offer them a free Bible. Over the years, Jake had somehow earned access to all kinds of places around town—hospitals, churches, street missions, seminaries, funeral homes. Folks just knew who he was and what he was about. At the prison, he would regularly move from cell to cell. "Brother, this doesn't look so good. No, not good, not good. You look pretty sad. Do you want to know how to become glad? We can fix your situation," he would say, holding out a Bible with a smile, enhanced by his perfect dentures.

"Go away old man!"

Completely undaunted, he would continue, "I understand, no problem, no problem. I'll see you next week." Jake had a lot of converts; he would just wear them down by a balanced combination of relentless persistence and genuine kindness. It was an effective approach.

This titan of a man was so interesting, I had to spend more time with him. I truly wanted to learn from him, so I made him an offer. I would bring a couple barbecue sandwiches to his midtown home each Thursday for lunch if we could just visit. One must understand that even late in life, Jake was very active, so this bargain was not a done deal. Thankfully he took me up on the offer, so for a number of months, we met at his home, ate some of Memphis's finest barbecue, and just talked, usually for a couple of hours. We talked about whatever we wanted to talk about. There was no plan. These get-togethers were so rich that once I asked Jake if I could record them. He kindly but quickly shut that idea down.

Big Jake wore his faith like one of his old, well-worn jackets. It just fit him. It was comfortable, it was functional, it was attractive, and it was genuine. During our lunches, sometimes he would talk about matters of faith. Other times he would not; it just depended. Once while we were both biting down on a couple Top's barbecue sandwiches with extra sauce and extra slaw, Jake spoke through the munching. "Durant, I thought I heard Gabriel blowing his horn for me the other night. I thought maybe it was time for me to go home." Jake had had a health scare that ended him up in the hospital. Then he smiled with his Pauline smile. "Nope, Gabriel wasn't blowing his horn for me; he was blowing his horn for Jed Stevens from across the street! Hee hee!" His neighbor had passed away! It just wasn't Jake's time to go, and he was perfectly fine with that. It was one of the few times that I've ever seen a person genuinely laughing about their own death.

To Jake, heaven was as real, maybe more real than that barbecue sandwich in his hands.

I pressed on a bit. "Are you ever afraid...of death that is."

He smiled through his ragged white beard that now had some sauce on it. "No, no way, no way!" Waving one hand loosely back and forth, he said, "Death has been defeated. Death has been put to death. That's what the gospel is all about. That's why it's Good News...It's God's great rescue plan." He smiled. "That's why Paul was able to mock death. He taunted death and the grave, 'Ha, where's your victory? How proud are you now? Hey, death, hey, where's your sting?' No, no way, we are not to fear death. It's just how we move on to the next state of our existence." He then turned his attention to a side order of baked beans on the coffee table, and that was that. For Jake, the mundane and the supernatural were always interlaced.

I was at Jake's funeral, and I can honestly say that I would not have wanted to be anywhere else on the planet. Fittingly, the eulogy was given by the kindly senior pastor who had passed Jake's theological acid test: "Are you born again?" Big Jake had such big faith, and heaven was so real and death so puny that his funeral was more like a going-away party. Knowing him well, for he was my grandfather, I am pretty certain that Jake would rather not have been recognized in this book, but he was also shrewd enough to leverage this chapter for the advancement of the kingdom of God. So, if I were to say to him, "Grandad, Jake, you get the last word. You get to say whatever you'd like to say at the conclusion of this chapter on faith and death," he'd smile at the peculiarity of the opportunity, think, and then with no hesitation, say, "Remember, you are but dust, and to dust you will return. Repent and believe the gospel."

CHAPTER 8

Deathbed Wisdom—How Should We Then Live?

"I made it all the way through World War II, fighting in the South Pacific without a scratch. I come home, and the first thing I know, I get put in a wheelchair by a drunk driver. How about that for luck?" Martin was one of those old-timers you could listen to all day. He was likeable, intelligent, and happy and had a prodigious memory. He was never in a hurry. He would tell you very candidly that he would have become bitter if it were not for his faith—bitter toward the Japanese, bitter toward the drunk driver, and bitter about the death of his first wife. I could not imagine Martin being bitter; he was always kind and always smiling.

About twenty years ago, I hosted a series of regular luncheons. Once a month, I would buy a tray of sandwiches, a gallon of iced tea, and some chips, and I would invite World War II veterans to come and share their stories. Usually about fifteen or twenty folks would attend, and often they would bring their sons to hear the tales of these humble heroes. I once pulled my son out of school to attend a luncheon. When I was asked why by the reluctant school's office, I told them, "To meet history." We heard firsthand accounts of men who had fought in the Battle of the Bulge, sailors who had seen combat off the coast of Iwo Jima, bomber squad members who had bombed Romanian oil refineries, and infantry-men who had fought their way across Europe.

Each month, I would invite a different veteran to tell their unique, personal story. Many of our guests were understandably reluctant and needed to be coaxed a bit to talk about these things. One man who had been blown off of a tank by a mine while hitching a ride through the Ardennes confessed at one of the luncheons, "This is not easy. It really isn't. This is not easy. I am telling you things that I have never told my wife." I knew that these ordinary men who did extraordinary things were dying off at an alarming rate and that their stories needed to be heard and their heroism needed to be acknowl-edged. They were aware of the same, so they graciously participated.

For some of the men, telling their stories was exceed-ingly difficult. I would assist them by asking simple, lead-ing questions about their time in basic training, and their experiences as they were transported to various parts of the world. We'd talk about the friends they made and their specific tasks or responsibilities during the war. These questions would help them to begin sharing about their military involvement, but the tone would darken, and the words did not flow easily when we began to ap-proach the topic of combat. Everything tightened up. The room would tighten up. The air got thicker. One gentleman, who was about eighty years old at the time, spoke staring through the lunch table as he was transported back through time to a battle in Belgium. Then he just stopped talking. Just stopped.

"Are you OK? You don't have to continue."

Taking a sip of water, he continued, "I need to do this for my friend." Under heavy artillery shelling, his friend had left the safety of their foxhole to assist another soldier, and as he did, he took a direct hit from a German shell and was vaporized. There was nothing left. When the smoke cleared, his friend was gone. The next day, his outfit was ordered to pull out, and that was that. These men had seen life and death, and it had shaped them, forged them into what we now call the Greatest Generation. Martin was one of these men.

At about nineteen, he found himself in the US Navy and on a ship that was part of a massive flotilla just off of the coast of Okinawa. It seemed the war may be coming to a costly end. On one hot and sticky morning, Martin's ship came under the attack from multiple kamikazes. Martin shared that there was no time to be afraid, as they were having to fend off three or four kamikazes at the same time.

"Sure, I was scared, but that came mostly after the fight. We were too busy. We just did what we were trained to do." As he manned a gun on the starboard side of the ship, a kamikaze came in low just over the water, almost level with his gun, which was pounding away. When the plane was just yards away, the young sailor dove behind the protective steel wall that surrounded the gun. He felt the ship shudder upon the impact. Through the noise, the heat, and the flames, he heard someone shouting the Lord's Prayer at the top of their lungs.

"Who is that shouting? Who is that screaming the Lord's Prayer?" Martin's mind was spinning. It was then he realized that the shouting was emanating from himself. He was the one yelling this prayer of hope in the midst of the deadly chaos. When he was almost crushed by war, prayer was what was left. He lived through the attack but confessed that it could have easily gone the other way. He was just not supposed to die that day.

After the luncheon, I had a chance to talk further with Martin. We continued our conversation after everyone had expressed their appreciation for his service as well as for his willingness to share his story. I asked Martin, who was very open to discussing these things, "Having lived such a full life and having experienced everything that you have experienced, what would you tell someone who is half your age and who is willing to learn more about what really matters in life? What would you tell them?"

He looked down and to the left as he readjusted himself in his wheelchair. "It's not complicated. Faith matters, whether you are staring into the canopy of a kamikaze or staring honestly at your own mortality. In the end, God is your only friend. Family is the most precious thing on earth, and it's our vocation to serve them at all costs. Be proud of your work. It is an honest expression of who you really are. Treat all people exactly the way you would like to be treated, and lastly, get used to change. Life is full of it. That's it. Like I said, it's not complicated. It really isn't."

Martin has passed on since we had this talk, but thankfully his words of wisdom have not.

Everyone's an Author—Writing Our Own Eulogies

First of all, thank you for taking the time to read this little book. I feel better now. For over twenty years, I have been carrying around these stories and their lessons in my heart. Now I can relax a bit knowing that they will not be lost, having been passed on to you.

Long ago, I learned as an educator that once you have truly learned something of value, you cannot unlearn it. If we have been genuinely stretched by a noble idea, our lives never truly return to their original proportions. To authentically know something of substance is to be changed, even if in the smallest way. The primary objective of this book was to pass along the wisdom of folk who were approaching the end of their lives, to secure their words to history. But there was another objective of this project: that this information might help shape us to be more thoughtful, deliberate, and caring people. These stories have challenged me for many years to be a better person, to live more fully, to be more grateful, and to strive to enjoy life every day. I must confess that these truths and the people behind them have had a substantial influence in my life, and I hope they will have a positive influence upon yours as well. I must also honestly confess that I have a long, long way to go as we grow on this journey. We just have to take it a step at a time.

As a pastor, I delivered many eulogies. I learned through doing this that ministers do not actually write a person's eulogy; they merely deliver them. The eulogy was already written by the person who is being remembered. Each day, we are adding a phrase, completing a sentence, editing a paragraph, adding another chapter, as we craft our own eulogies by the way we live our lives each moment. It is my hope that this book will help you as you write yours. Again, thank you sincerely for taking the time to think about these things.

T. Durant Fleming

Dr. T. Durant Fleming, Author of *Splendid Agony: Celebrating Dyslexia*

Durant, who was raised and educated in Memphis, knew something was amiss when his parents sat him down to inform him that he would be repeating the third grade. To Durant, the third grade was a painful blur and one thing was certain, this strong willed, dyslexic child wanted nothing to do with school, ever again. So, he considered running way. Anything would have been better than to return to those sterile classrooms with the real struggle and confusion that was associated with them.

Durant did return to the third grade again, but this time he had the dedicated support of his loving parents, his passionate teachers, his enthusiastic coaches, tenacious reading specialists, and his three academically inclined brothers. As a result of the critical support he received, Durant stumbled forward, on through elementary school and into middle school, then he began to gain academic traction during high school. Completing his undergraduate degree in Communications, he happily gathered three Masters degrees, and earned his doctorate by the time he was thirty. He then went on to become a career educator, first as a teacher, a vice principal, then as a Head of School. He laughs now about having the ability to run a school, but not being able to recall the school's phone number when asked.

He spent a large part of his adult life in the very classrooms he once loathed. When asked about his academic accomplishments, he once replied, "In those early years I had incredible support, a number of people truly invested in me and it changed my life forever. Also, I discovered that my dyslexia was actually a benefit, the very condition that almost drove me to despair as a child became my greatest academic ally. I wouldn't trade it for the world, it's a fantastic gift."

After many years in the educational world, often working with students with dyslexia, their teachers, and families, Durant decided that it was time to write, *Splendid Agony: Celebrating Dyslexia*. This easy-to-read book offers a unique glimpse into the dyslexic mind, it draws from many poignant stories from Durant's journey, and offers practical principles to effectively support students with dyslexia. This encouraging book was specifically written to support teachers, learning specialists, and especially the parents of dyslexic learners.

Durant and his wife Sharon now live in the beautiful hills of North Central Arkansas with their spunky miniature Schnauzers, Archie and Phoebe. Durant enjoys writing, fly fishing, playing the bagpipes, cooking, and photography. He is presently planning on building the perfect fishing boat in his garage. When asked, "Why did you write this book?" His answer is simple, "Because other people helped me, and that made all of the difference."

When I Was Twenty

When I was twenty, I'd live forever.
At thirty, life was always ahead.
At forty, curiously halfway done.
At fifty, plenty of funerals.
At sixty, grateful for every day.
I no longer assume I'll see tomorrow.
—T. D. F.